Pieces

by Jim Branch

Go inward. Search for the reason that bids you write; find out whether it is spreading out its roots in the deepest places of your heart, acknowledge to yourself whether you would have to die if it were denied you to write. This above all—ask yourself in the stillest hour of your night: must I write? Delve into your heart for a deep answer. And if this should be affirmative, if you may meet this earnest question with a strong and simple "I must," then build your life according to this necessity; your life even into its most indifferent and slightest hour must be a sign of this urge and testimony to it.

~ Rainer Maria Rilke

This little collection of thoughts, poems, and prayers are just the meanderings of the Spirit in my life through the years. My hope is that these movements of God within my heart and soul, might actually be of some help to you and your journey as well. I would suggest using this book as a kind of "day book." You might consider reading only one or two *Pieces* a day, then just sitting with them, reflecting on them, and paying attention to God's Spirit within them—and see if that sparks anything of the life of the Spirit within you.

Grace and Peace,

JB

Thoughts

Balance

When most of us think of the word *balance,* we think
of a life with equal amounts (or right amounts) of everything—a life in
which our work and play and family and friendships and faith all receive
comparable amounts of attention and energy. In the spiritual life, however,
the word balance must be defined differently. As a matter of fact the word
balance might not be the most appropriate word to use at all—the word
centered might be more accurate. Because in the life of faith, balance
means having Christ as the center around which everything else revolves.
Thus, life is only balanced when everything is centered on Christ. Christ is
the hub of the wheel; the focal point of our lives that allows life to function
the way it was created to function. So the question becomes not *"Do I
have enough of God in my life?"* but *"Is Christ the center of my life? What
does my life revolve around?"* The answer to these questions will tell me a
lot about whether my life is truly balanced or not.

Naked

Naked. How does that word make you feel? What is the first response that comes up from within you? Terror? Embarrassment? Anxiety? Shame? Or does it bring about more positive feelings? Freedom? Intimacy? Delight? I have to admit that my first response is closer to terror than anything else. Even the mention of the word makes me want to grab for cover. Because at my fearful core being naked means being exposed and uncovered—which seems so unsafe. It means being seen for who and what I really am, not just who I project myself to be. And surely if anyone were ever to see me completely naked it would most certainly lead to rejection. Thus the very idea of being naked leads to overwhelming amounts of fear and insecurity.

But there is another side to this story. Because somewhere deep within me (and really within all of us I believe) there is a longing for nakedness—a nakedness that we were created both in and for. It is the kind of nakedness mentioned in Genesis where we are told that the man and woman *were both naked and unashamed.* They were totally known and yet totally loved. What a beautiful picture of our deepest hopes and wildest dreams: total vulnerability and total acceptance. This is the kind of nakedness we were made for. This is the kind of nakedness that gives us a hint of the type of relationship God longs for with each of us; and the type of relationship God longs for each of us to offer one another.

Gathering

Gather the pieces that are left over. Let nothing be wasted. (John 6:12)
The call came at about 9:30 pm on a typical Thursday evening in early December. I had just returned home from somewhere or other and was talking with my wife in the living room about the events of the day when our oldest son called on his cell phone to ask if he could go to the church coffee shop with some friends. As she spoke to him there was an abrupt halt in the conversation—a significant amount of panic and anxiety filled her usually calm face. Our oldest son, as his mother was listening, had just been involved in an automobile accident. I quickly got news of his location and headed for the door—not being able to get there fast enough. Fears and prayers consumed the drive until I reached the scene. As I arrived I saw him—in one piece, unhurt—standing with a few friends in the midst of the broken glass and police lights and passersby. My only desire at that moment was wrap my arms around him—which I did as he began to express his sorrow and sadness. "I'm so sorry. I'm so sorry," was all he could say; which was met only by my relief and gratitude that he was unhurt.

"I'm just so glad you are okay."

So we stood there in the middle of the road and waited as reports were written and information was exchanged and wrecker services were called. Looking down at my feet all I could see was broken pieces… glass, plastic, metal, etc. The pieces were littering the street—such an appropriate description of the scene in general—broken. Broken glass. Broken pieces. Broken hearts. Broken world. Broken.

That's when the words came. Words that I had been captured by months before that were returning at just the right time. *"Gather the pieces that are left over. Let nothing be wasted."* Words that offered such comfort and hope. Words that spoke of God's heart and God's presence even in the midst of the broken pieces of this life. It was as if Jesus was saying to me, "I am here. I am with you even in the brokenness. Gather the pieces and you will find me. You are not alone in this. With me nothing is wasted. I will use even the most broken situations to mold and make you into the amazing creation that I have always longed for you to be."

What a crazy world this is that we live in—a world where brokenness is unfortunately a part of life. Death and suffering, war and violence, conflict and strife…from anger, hatred, and racism to hurricanes, tornados and tsunamis. We can't avoid it or deny it, no matter how hard we may try. But the beautiful thing is that brokenness does not have the last word…wholeness does. For no matter how broken the heart, or the life, or the circumstance; we have this amazing God who says, "With me nothing is wasted. Gather the pieces, I am in the midst of them."

Fear

The older I get, the more I realize that quite possibly the biggest single enemy of our spiritual lives (other than Satan himself) is fear. Fear seems to be at the very core of all the things that battle against my heart and soul. At the core of my busyness is fear. At the core of my insecurity is fear. At the core of my anxiety is fear. At the core of my competitiveness…you guessed it—fear. Fear of not having what it takes. Fear of not having any value. Fear of not being lovable. The list goes on and on.

And maybe the main reason this enemy is so strong and dangerous is that by and large it is a hidden enemy. We never really look beneath the surface of our more familiar enemies to spot it. We rarely follow any of these foes down far enough to see what is at their root. And when we don't know what we are really fighting, how can we possibly be victorious? We just keep getting defeated over and over again. This fear robs us of the intimacy we were created for. It robs us of the freedom that God longs for us to enjoy. It robs us of genuinely loving relationships. It simply controls the way we live our lives.

What are we to do? How can we possibly fight against this? A first step would seem to be identifying and *naming* our fears. Somehow naming our fears takes some of their power away to control us. Ann Lamott once said, "When you make friends with fear, it can't rule you." Once our enemy is identified it makes it much easier to wage war.

Secondly, we need to remember that our real enemy (Satan) is the "father of lies." He will use his lies to manipulate us into believing whatever he can. Because of this, it seems that we need to ask ourselves, "What lies are we believing that are simply not true? How is our seeing or thinking distorted?" When the disciples were on the sea battling against the storm (Mark 6:45-52) they screamed out in terror because they thought Jesus was a ghost. Now it wasn't really a ghost upon the water… they just thought it was. It was their distorted thinking and seeing that gave power to their fears. Once they saw things clearly and therefore thought about things more accurately—they were able to put everything in perspective.

Which brings us to the biggest weapon we have been given to wage war against fear—and that is what John calls "perfect love" (1 John 4:18). It is perfect love that puts everything in perspective for us. Once the voice of perfect love calls out to us, "Take courage. It is I. Don't be afraid." Then we are reminded that the love of the one who made us, and called us into being, and cares for us more than we can even care for ourselves is in control of all things. And His heart for us is good—he can be trusted even when circumstances look dire because he loves us so immensely and completely. When he speaks His words of affection and peace and we hear and truly believe them; then we know that if he is with us—it will be well. Whatever it is, whatever the seas look like, it will be well.

Stories

Immediately after my calling—without consulting anyone around me and without going up to Jerusalem to confer with those who were apostles long before I was—I got away to Arabia. Later I returned to Damascus, but it was three years before I went up to Jerusalem **to compare stories** *with Peter. (Galatians 1:16-18)*

I love that the first thing Paul and Peter did when they got together, for the very first time, was tell stories. Can you imagine being a fly on the wall? There is something about the telling of our stories (or of God's story in us) that is very rich and life giving; it's almost like the stories *must* be told in order to have their fully desired effect in our hearts and lives and souls. And the funny thing is that I'm not sure who they have the bigger impact on, the *hearer* or the *teller*. Obviously there is something wonderful about *hearing* stories of how God grabbed someone's heart or made someone whole; but there is also this strange and wonderful dynamic that takes place in the heart of the *teller* even as the story is being told. It is as if somehow it is continuing to move and to grow in his heart and soul even as he shares what he has seen or heard. Do you know what I'm talking about? It's those times when you are in the middle of telling some incredible story of God's Spirit and God's work, and you actually begin to *hear* what you are saying…and be completely captured by it. It is almost as if you didn't completely realize what all was going on until you began to tell it, and as you opened your mouth it is almost as if the story began telling itself and was just using your mouth as its vehicle. After all, it is not your story, or even mine (or theirs for that matter), but the story of God. It is His, and something about its quality tells us that. Somehow if the story was only about me, or about you, it wouldn't carry the same weight; it wouldn't have the same impact. It would fall lifeless to the ground and die—so many of my stories have suffered that fate through the years simply because I didn't yet understand that the story wasn't about me, but about Him. Stories about Him have life; they live on and produce their fruit long after their telling. It is simply beautiful.

I have had the pleasure of experiencing this a lot this through the years, as one story after another has simply unfolded before my very eyes; as if the story itself was somehow longing to be seen and heard…and told. I'm just grateful for the grace (and it is completely grace) to pay attention and to recognize even a little of what He was up to at the moment. Thanks be to God!

Room

We throw open our doors to God and discover at the same moment that he has already thrown open his door to us. We find ourselves standing where we always hoped we might stand—out in the wide open spaces of God's grace and glory, standing tall and shouting our praise. (Romans 5:2 - The Message)

I read these words the other day and just can't get away from them, they have continued to echo and reverberate deeply within me. I guess that's because the idea of spaciousness has been one I have always been drawn to. Maybe it's because of the freedom (and life and grace) that is inherent in a spacious place. A spacious place offers room; room to roam, room to grow, room to flourish, room to be…and room to become. I like room, I don't like to be crowded or constricted or restrained. And I don't just like room, I need room…the life of God within me requires it. It seems to me that the very life of the Spirit is one of spaciousness, ever expanding us within. The more deeply we journey into God, the more room there is, and the more spacious and free life becomes. I like that…I like it a lot. It is so inviting. It makes me want to throw my doors completely open to him; knowing that when I do, I find his doors already wide open before me—with the wide open spaces of his grace and love going on and on and on. What could be more inviting than that?

Being With

I pray that out of his glorious riches he may strengthen you with power through his Spirit in your inner being, so that Christ may dwell in your hearts through faith. (Ephesians 3:16-17)

There is a definite art to *being with* someone. It involves being fully present to them—open and attentive. It consists of listening to them and offering them space and room to be. It requires that we not be occupied or preoccupied with other people or things, and ultimately asks us to let go of our agendas and control. *Being with* someone involves and investment of time and focused stillness; it is one of the most important disciplines in all of the spiritual life.

Paul prays that the Ephesians might have a deep work of the Spirit go on within them, so that Christ might dwell in their hearts through faith. The word that Paul uses for *dwell* is the word used for a permanent and durable residence—not a short-term and temporary condition, but a lasting and enduring state. This *dwelling* has to do with the art of *with-ness*; God *being with* us and us, in turn, learning to *be with* Him. It requires a bit of a shift from our normal mode of operation; a shift from doing to being. It's almost as if Paul knew that we all have a tendency to take the outside-in approach to the life of faith—to think of it in terms of behavior modification and sin management—when the truth is that faith is in actuality an inside-out process. True transformation does not start with doing and then somehow magically impact being. It starts with being and then works its way out into doing. The work of the Spirit is a deep work of the heart that always finds its way out into the way we live our lives. That's how genuine transformation takes place.

Prayer

But when you pray, go into your room, close the door and pray to your Father, who is unseen. Then your Father, who sees what is done in secret, will reward you. And when you pray, do not keep on babbling like pagans, for they think they will be heard because of their many words. Do not be like them... (Matthew 6:6-7)

I've always had a sneaking suspicion that there is much more to most things than meets the eye—prayer for instance. For years I was under the impression that prayer consisted of closing your eyes, bowing your head, and talking to God. The pictures and images of prayer that I carried around in my heart and mind, quite frankly, left much to be desired. Prayer was not an activity I was particularly drawn to or excited about. My guess is that this had much more to do with my definition of prayer than it did with the real practice of prayer. It wasn't until much later in life that I began to see that maybe my definition of prayer was far too small and rigid. Prayer wasn't so much about performing a duty as it was about building a wonderfully intimate relationship. Prayer was not simply throwing all the words I can muster at the unseen God, but it—at its very core—has always been about union with the God who lives within us. I think that's what Jesus is really getting at in Matthew 6; he is trying to recapture the true meaning and practice of prayer, which is simply being with God.

Don't stand on street corners, don't babble on and on; prayer is much more intimate and personal than that. Instead go into your closet—that space where true intimacy is possible—and shut the door. Leave everyone and everything else on the outside; I want it to be just me and you. I want us to be together in a way and a place where I have your undivided attention. I have so much I want to say to you; so much of me that I want you to know. And this space and time is the place where that is most possible; the place where I can have the deepest desires of my heart fulfilled, which is just to be with you, my Beloved. Come inside where things are still and quiet and you can hear every whisper of my loving Spirit deep within your heart and soul. That's prayer.

"Here's what I want you to do: Find a quiet, secluded place so you won't be tempted to role-play before God. Just be there as simply and honestly as you can manage. The focus will shift from you to God, and you will begin to sense his grace." (Matthew 6:6 The Message)

Centered

Do any human beings ever realize life while they live it?—every, every minute? (from the play **Our Town** *by Thornton Wilder)*

What a question…a great, great question. Do they? Do we? Do I? It seems that if I did, it would make a world of difference in the way I went about living that life every day. It would affect the *who* and the *what* and particularly the *how* of every single minute of every single day. A few years ago I was sitting with a dear friend at my favorite table in my favorite restaurant and a similar question bubbled to the surface: "Are you living the life you want to live?" Of course the question was not about winning the lottery or living in a house on the beach, but more about, "In the life and the place you have been given, are you living the quality of life that you really want to live?" It is a question, not so much of circumstance, but of depth and quality, of priority and investment. And as we sat with that question and considered it deeply another question followed on its heels…"If not, why not?" Sometimes we live our lives feeling more like our lives are living us instead. Feeling like our life and our world is filled with things we really have no choice about; running frantically and busily from one thing to the next, out of control. I think that's what Jesus was addressing at Martha's house (Luke 10). Martha was distracted. The word for distracted, I am told, in this context can be more descriptively translated "to drag around." Martha was feeling drug around. She had no choice…after all look at all that "has to be" done. But Jesus always has a much different perspective, a different way of seeing and of being. Look at what Jesus has to say to her: *"Martha, Martha," the Lord answered, "you are worried and upset about many things, but few things are needed—or indeed only one. Mary has chosen what is better, and it will not be taken away from her" (Luke 10:41).* It is almost as if Jesus is saying, "Martha, dear Martha, you are missing it. Realize life while you are living it. See what is truly primary and what is only secondary; what needs to be foreground and what has to be kept in the background; what is important versus what is merely urgent. Do not center your life on circumstances, or on duty, or need, or reputation, or agenda…center your life on me. Everything else, including the *"to do list,"* will take care of itself. You are worried and upset about many things…why is that? Come to me, the one needed thing—the best thing. Be with me, sit at my feet, listen to my words, look into my eyes, and allow the rest of your life to be determined by that."

Faith

What does the word *faith* mean? Many have tried to define it. The writer of the book of Hebrews says it is "being sure of what we hope for and certain of what we do not see" (Hebrews 11:1). A. W. Tozer says that faith is "the gaze of the soul on a loving God" (*The Pursuit of God*). Martin Luther called faith "the yes of the heart." And Frederick Buechner says that faith is "the direction your feet start moving when you find that you are loved."

But maybe there is no better definition of the word *faith* than the one offered in the fourth chapter of John (verse 50). It says the royal official "took Jesus at his word." What a great definition of faith. Believing that what God has said is true. Being convinced. Convinced that he loves us the way he says he does. Convinced that he is in control and can be trusted with our lives. Convinced that he will truly care for us and those we love. Convinced that his heart for us is good. Convinced.

Is there a place in your life right now where you are having to walk by faith? A place where you are having to believe that God's heart for you is good even though you have a hard time seeing it in the circumstances? What does it mean for you to "take Jesus at his word" right now?

A Do-Over

Did you ever wish you could have a do-over? You know, like when you get to the end of a conversation or an event and you think, "I really missed it there." As a matter of fact, in your desire to be helpful—to whoever it was that you were speaking to or sitting with—you were actually anything but that. The desire was a wonderful thing, and came from a beautiful place, but it actually kept you from creating the space for them *to be*. For some reason you talked a little too much and listened a little too little, so that the time became more about you than about them. So, you look back and long for another chance, not for your sake but for theirs. Because what they were really looking for and hoping for was just someone to be with them; and your misguided desire kept you from being able to do that. Luckily God is big enough to use even our bumbling and our fumbling to accomplish His purposes. I guess that's some consolation, huh? Plus the fact that next time, I'll know better…I hope.

A New Normal

you let men ride over our heads;
we went through fire and through water;
yet you have brought us out to a place of abundance.
(Psalm 66:12)

You *let* it happen—this *riding over our heads*—whoever or whatever it may
have been. You didn't cause it…but you could have stopped it. I mean, I
know it doesn't happen every day, but I have seen you spring into action
and miraculously come to someone's aid or defense; come to protect or
deliver. And yet, for some reason, in this case you didn't. You allowed *it*.
Does that mean you sat idly by and watched? Or does it mean
that—although the brokenness of this world is its cause—that you are big
enough to bring beauty out of the tragedy? You saw it coming, and *let* it
stand, because of what you knew it would do within us. You knew that the
groaning it would produce would have an effect on us like nothing else
could or would. So where exactly were you when we were going through
the fire; being consumed by the agonizing flames of grief or sadness or
mourning or pain? What were you doing while the mighty waters rushed
over us and swept us away; as we struggled and fought to survive—to
keep our heads above water? Were you with us in some mysteriously
hidden way that we were not able to completely comprehend at the time?
Were you in the midst of the fire with us; shielding us from the fury of the
flames? Were you in the middle of the raging currents beside us; holding
and sustaining us—keeping us afloat? After all, you know what the
groaning is like; in fact, you know it like no other. Did it break your heart to
have to watch the *riding over* us unfold; to know the depths of the pain we
were going through, and not intervene? How hard that must have been for
you.
    When we are in the midst of the groan it is hellish. It is hard to believe,
or even consent to the fact that something good might possibly result from
the chaos and brokenness. Much less to think that it could be some
strange path to a place called *abundance*—that is almost unimaginable.
Yet all of us, on the backside of the *riding over*, usually have to admit that
something took place within us—or among us—that could have happened
no other way. We would never have chosen the path in a million
years—not then, and most likely not again—but we can't deny the beauty
of the new place at which we eventually arrived. How in the world did we
get here? Who would've imagined that the groans and cries and tears and
struggle would have brought us to this place; this place where our hearts
have been both broken and expanded, where our souls have been both
crushed and deepened beyond measure. Who could've dreamt that the

effect of the fire and of the water would have been to make us more like Jesus—he who *suffers with* and delivers; he who *weeps over* and heals?

There has been a lot of groaning going around lately. It seems to be coming from every direction. I guess it is true that "each one of us sits beside a pool of tears." And it is so hard to watch the groaners groan and the mourners mourn and the strugglers struggle and not be able to do anything to help. It is so tempting to try to come to the rescue, but rescue is not really possible, or even preferable...because something much deeper is going on. In the words of Gerald May, "There is no way out, only through." Something deep and wonderful happens in the *going through*. So we must resist the urge to provide an escape—if that were even possible—because the struggle, or the groaning, or the grief, or the pain is the very thing that is able to do a beautiful work within. All there is for us to do is trust. Trust that God really is in control. Trust that God really is up to something, in spite of all appearances. Trust that God really is big enough to sustain, to comfort, to deliver, to heal...and ultimately to transform. Trust that through the fire and through the water lies *a place of abundance*.

Intimacy

As I sit and hold my 10 month old son, his eyes totally fixed on mine, indiscernible sounds of love streaming from his lips...I am amazed (again) at such love, such connection, such relationship, such intimacy—with no words required. This is what I was made for (I feel it in the very core of my soul) by a God who shows Himself, by His very nature, to be a God of intimate relationship.

What a wonderfully terrifying thing to realize; that the very nature of the Creator is one of total intimacy. The first part of John tells us that the Word was *with* God—toward God, facing God. The very essence of the relationship between God and the Word is one of connection, intimacy, relationship ... face-to-face communication. What a joy it is to know that He is wonderfully able to meet the needs of His children for connection and deep relationship.

It is wonderful because only One that has experienced total intimacy can give us hope for a similar state of existence for ourselves. And it is terrifying because of the very idea of being face-to-face with One who can see into my very soul—no protection, no hiding, no masks, just the real me—completely vulnerable. It strikes fear in my heart; fear of being seen by God— inadequate, ugly, real, afraid I won't measure up. I don't, however, have to measure up; for God's eyes are not like mine. He looks lovingly and longingly at His children more deeply even than I look at my own, as I stand over their beds at night with a heart bursting so with love that I can't keep my hands from their hair or my lips from their cheeks. He looks at me and sees His Son, His Beloved, and desires that I sit facing Him through all of the seconds, hours, days, and years of my life...uttering whatever indiscernible sounds of love and affection that are at my disposal.

As I can readily see in my children, I was created for intimacy. I can't, however, expect to be truly connected with anyone until I am able to be truly connected with Jesus. My capacity for intimacy (with spouse, child, or friend) comes directly from Him and His desire that I experience the joys of true connectedness (John 15:7). And oh what a gift...those few seconds, minutes or hours when *True Intimacy* breaks through the isolation of our ordinary lives to grace (and I know it's grace) us with Its (His) presence ... those are moments to savor...to sit and marvel over.

Between

Recently I have found myself captured by a gospel passage that has come to life for me…again. It is the coming of Jesus to the disciples on the sea (in Matthew 14:22-33). It is a truly incredible story—one that has spoken to me often through the years in a multitude of ways. But there has been one particular aspect of this story that has been a wonderful source of reflection for me lately. It involves that sacred space that Jesus invites Simon Peter to step out into. It is the space between…between the boat and Jesus… between letting go and being taken hold of…between the old and familiar and the new and unknown…between control and agenda and dependence and detachment. It is a space that is both completely terrifying and unbelievably exciting. It is the space before your answer has come or your problem has been fixed. It is the space where you must trust the heart of God alone for your life. It is the space of genuine transformation.

Wholeness

Few words in all of the Old Testament are as rich as the Hebrew word *shalom*. As a matter of fact, the translations of this one little word are varied and numerous—trying in vain to capture the fullness of the idea it is meant to communicate. The most common translation we have for the word is *peace*, but that does not seem to go far enough. Therefore, it is also translated *prosperity, tranquility, well-being, safety*, and *security*. Maybe the best word we have in the English language, however, that even comes close to capturing the true essence of *shalom* is the word *wholeness*. Because at its core *shalom* is about experiencing the creation intent of God. *Shalom* is life as God intended it to be—life before sin and brokenness. *Shalom* is finding our way back into the garden where we were created to enjoy and experience God in His fullness as we "walk with Him in the cool of the day." It is what our souls are really and truly longing for—deep communion and connection and intimacy with our God.

Downward

In our day and in our culture the language of *ascent* has indeed become a popular one. Success, productivity, power, independence, and competition seem to be held up, even in the Christian community, as characteristics to be valued and pursued. But when we listen carefully to the voice of Scripture and the words of our Savior, we begin to get a sense of a language and an attitude that is very different from that of the world around us. Jesus, in fact, used a completely different vocabulary to talk about life and faith. He used words like service, fruitfulness, humility, dependence, and compassion—most of which run directly against the grain of both the culture and the day. In fact, when it comes to the language of the Kingdom it seems that the word *descent* might actually be a more appropriate choice. Hence, if we really wish to follow Jesus' example and his teaching, we may find that the way actually leads downward.

Groaning

It seems like so much of the life of faith has to do with *groaning*—both the groaning of our own hearts and the groaning of the heart of our God. It is a groaning that comes from a deep longing for all to be as it was intended. It is that place where we fully embrace our sadness and frustration that all is not as it was designed to be, rather than try to escape, avoid, or deny it. It is that place where we acknowledge that the world has gone terribly wrong, it is filled with decay and death and suffering and sadness and pain. It is that place where we acknowledge that somehow God meets us in some beautifully mysterious way right in the midst of it all. He meets us in a way that we couldn't be met otherwise—making this groaning both an embracing of where we are, as well as a deep longing more—for deliverance, for restoration, for wholeness. Therefore, the life of faith is a life in which we watch and wait and long and hope for the Creator to finally intervene; for him to come and set everything right once again; for him to enter into this world and restore all things to their creation intent.

Dying

I'm learning a lot about dying lately…and I hate it. I'm terrible at it. I would probably never choose it on my own, it is usually chosen for me. And I resist it almost all the time. But it's just unavoidable.

Currently I am living smack dab in the center of Holy Week, walking the road to the cross with Jesus, knowing that much of the life I have lived (and loved) up to this point has been torn away, that on the horizon a cross awaits, and that there is some kind of new life and resurrection on the other side of it all.

But right now the cross is looming, the sadness of loss and the stench of death keep me from the joy and excitement of what is to come. I'm convinced that whatever it is will be beautiful, but there is still more dying left to do before I can get there.

Small

For quite some time I have been living with the suspicion that God has a preference for the small, the hidden, the quiet, and the lowly. I see it clearly all over the pages of Scripture, but maybe nowhere more clearly than in the Christmas narrative. To imagine that God, the Creator of all that is, chose to enter into that creation in the way that he did is simply astounding. To come into this world as a tiny, helpless baby; born to a couple of poor teenagers, who could afford nothing more that a lowly stable for a room, is beyond my imagination. It is almost as if God wanted to slip into our world without being noticed at all; except by those that were watching and waiting, by those paying extra careful attention.

So, during this season of Advent and Christmas, would it not be wise of us to try and take notice of the small, the hidden, the quiet, and the ordinary? Would it not be wise to ask ourselves, "If God chose to become smaller (in some amazingly mysterious way that we cannot fully comprehend), then how might he be asking us to become smaller as well?" And who knows, if we keep asking ourselves that very question, and if we are really fortunate, then maybe, just maybe, by the end of the week we might actually have become small enough for Christ to arrive; both among us and within us.

New

New is something we all deeply long for. In fact, which one of us is not excited about a new beginning, or a clean slate, or a new lease on life, or a brand new heart? Who among us is not thrilled at the prospect of all the old and the worn out and the broken being done away with in favor of the new and the fresh and the whole. But I'll be the first to admit that as much as I yearn for all things to be made new, I don't want it to cost me anything. I don't want it to be a process that is slow and difficult and arduous and long. I want it to just suddenly appear, to be as quick and as easy as possible—like waving some sort of magic wand.

New birth, however, does not come easy. In fact, the birthing process is often a long and painful one. I guess that's why they call it labor. And the necessity of this *labor* is not only true of physical birth, but of spiritual birth as well. That does not mean that we can somehow work our way into some new state of being or of seeing. The new thing, whatever it may be, must be *conceived* in us, and that is something that we ultimately have no control over—no more control than Mary had as the Spirit *came upon her*. The *birthing* of this new thing, however, is a different story. The birthing process, the process of bringing this new thing into existence, requires a labor—a labor that is likely filled with much pain and turmoil and struggle. A pain and a turmoil and a struggle that is offset, however, by the overwhelming joy of seeing this new thing being brought into existence—being born either among us or within us. Therefore, it is a labor that is both purposeful and hopeful. It is a labor that, to borrow a phrase from a popular song, is *a labor of love*.

Poems

ache

sometimes
all that is within me
is an ache
that cannot be named
yet cannot be dismissed
it has something to say
and needs to be heard
so
all i can do
is hold it up
as prayer
and trust
that somehow
it makes perfect sense
to you

awakening

shaking off the slumber
raising an eyelid
peeking out from under the covers

rolling over
checking the clock
closing my eyes again
too comfortable
too warm

just five more minutes
and then i will awaken
…so I snooze

you would think sleeping
was better than living

and life passes by
missed
because eyes are closed

sleeping is so easy
           so warm
           so safe

wake up
don't sleep your life away
the day awaits
with all its beauty
and all of its wonder
and all of its mystery

so come awake within me
o my soul
come awake

bare

the covering
has gone
shed its leaves
all that is left is
what is
the true essence of
the thing itself
in all of its twistedness
and all of its beauty
like a tree in winter
this heart
laid bare

bestowed

dancing madly
for applause
to achieve a sense of *me*
and yet
can *me* be gained by effort
or must it be a gift
only to be received

canyon

standing at the base of the canyon
looking up
how immense the walls
towering far above
and how deep the floor
dark and hopeless
it seems an impossible climb
out of this pit of sadness
groaning and despair
how can i possibly reach the other side
where life can continue
once again?

how can i do this?
i cry into the chasm
how can i do this?
it just doesn't seem possible

i need someone
who knows the way
through the pain and darkness
the despair and loneliness
back to life again
who could possibly know the way?
only one who has been there
who has been to the depths
and made it back alive
only one who has seen rock bottom
and survived even still

i need someone who knows the way
and can walk beside me
through the darkest night
back into the light again

only you can offer hope
you alone
hold the possibility
that in spite of all the pain
life can one day begin again

only you can offer hope
that the canyon rim
can someday be reached

only you know the way
so reach down
from on high
and take hold
of this broken heart
reach down
to the bottom of this abyss
and lift me up
take me
in your strong and tender arms
and make my shattered life
whole once again

changes

change and fear
must be related somehow
either sisters, brothers,
or second cousins once removed
good friends at the very least

they hang out in the same places
they live in the same neighborhood
maybe even on the same block
they eat at each other's table
and seem to enjoy each other's company

thinking of one will likely lead to the other
when one comes the other is not far behind
tagging along, clinging to a shirttail

are these two inseparable?
or does it just feel that way?

contemplation

what is this that stirs within?
willing to guide if i will listen
a faint whisper   yet not

an almost imperceptible knowing
awakened from a sleep
in which One is calling softly

knowing
but not sure how
hearing
but not sure when
dreaming?

as a soft voice in a sleeping child's ear
knowing to the depths what was whispered
and the delight of the Whisperer

deep inside

way down
under the layers
of activity and insecurity
a heart
covered over

longing to be known
to be lived from
to have its truth honored

but the journey to its core
is a long one
requiring much
time and
effort and
courage

maybe life on the surface is easier
safer
or is it?
is it really life at all?
or only slow death?

for the true contents of this heart
must be discovered
must be nurtured
must be known
must be released
must be lived
must be

for what is real
and true
and good
is deep inside

deepening

the flow is continuous
ever-present within
gently forming its path—over time
without extravagance or attention
yet constantly shaping and deepening
its way in the heart
not trying, just flowing

mine is to surrender
to the path of the flow
letting the water have its way
making me into what i am becoming

deeper still

dark and deep
no bottom in sight
endless amounts of insecurity
bubble up from its depths
more than seems possible

where does it come from?
this fear of nothingness?
it just keeps coming
                    and coming
                            and coming

but you
aren't scared away
you don't shake your head
because you know
that you are
deeper still

your love is higher
    than my greatest fears
and longer
    than my list of inadequacies
and wider
    than my longing for worth
and deeper
    than my deepest darkness
greater
    than all my need
hard to imagine
    but true

for yes, my darkness is deep
but your love is
deeper still

divide

i have separated
my mind and my heart
much to my detriment

heart talks mind into
believing things
it should know better than

feeling leads thinking
down a false road
in the wrong direction
but has convinced him
that it is right
because it feels like it is

how can mind be so easily swayed
so easily fooled
so easily seduced

this is what happens
when mind and heart
are separated
when they operate independently
a house divided
which cannot stand

the two must be reunited
wed once more
and anchored
to truth

truth that will
set me free

door

the door is open
but i am hesitant

"move on through" says the voice
"the other side has much to offer"

but instead i stop in the middle
        afraid to enter
        afraid of the cost
        afraid of the journey to the other side

moving through definitely has its price
but the price of not moving seems higher
for on the other side
        of doubt lies faith
        of despair lies hope
        of disappointment lies love
        of sorrow lies joy
        of mourning lies dancing
        of struggle lies growth
        of brokenness lies wholeness

"so move on through" says the voice
"for the other side has much to offer"

yet i am still hesitant
and still the door is open

easter

the silence was deafening
that early morning as she stood,
gripped by a love that would not release her
everyone else was gone
back to their homes and their families

"how could they forget so quickly?" she thought
as she stood in the first light of dawn,
tears streaming down her cheeks
"did they not feel it too...the love?"
"if they did, how could they leave?"

her heart would not allow her to go
so she stayed—as near to him as she knew how
was she waiting?
was she hoping?
or was she simply doing the only thing she could
to be near the place he was last near
she would rather be near him than anyone or anything
so she stayed...and cried
longing to hear her name from his lips once more

and then suddenly the voice...it startled her
looking through the tears she could not see who it was

"have you seen him?" she asked
"do you know where he is?"

it wasn't until he uttered her name
that she recognized his voice
and at its sweet sound
everything in her was raised to life again
it was easter you see...and he had risen
and because of that
so had she

eyes

that search to and fro
that saw my unformed substance
that are on the sparrow
that see my heart
that know me through and through
that weep over my hurt
that watch and wait
that leap with delight at my return

show me your eyes
and it will be enough
for when i see them
i see your affection
because your eyes
can't hide your feelings
for me

gathering

scattered pieces littering the hillside
scraps from what once fed multitudes
casualties of the train wreck of provision and need
leftovers, unwanted, discarded, useless
or so it seems

a death; a loss; a heartbreak
a wound; a brokenness; a darkness
loneliness; despair; isolation
the scattered pieces of this life
littering the ground of my being
unwanted; unwelcome; uninvited
fit only to be mourned and thrown away
or so it seems

until touched by the hand of one
who brings beauty from ashes
who utters the words of life and hope
"gather all the broken pieces"
weaving the fragments of my brokenness
into the me that was planned from the beginning

"let nothing be wasted"
and suddenly that which seemed to have no value
becomes meaningful and beautiful in your care
these parts make a whole
they serve a divine purpose

"I will rescue the lame and gather what has
been scattered"
and make it into a vital part of you;
the object of my great delight and affection

so sing and shout
brighten up and spin around
for I am gathering your pieces
and restoring you
into a fearful and wonderful creation
and nothing will be wasted

giggle

i can't stifle the giggle
when your mouth draws close to my ear
whispers of affection
light up my heart
and then my face
they make me beam
others see and think it odd
but they don't hear
they don't feel your breath upon them
if they did, they'd giggle too

grasping

something is terribly wrong within her
a long slow bleeding of her heart and soul
has been her constant companion
for as long as she can remember
so many things
she has tried
to make the bleeding stop
or to make her feel better
for at least a moment
but the long line of solutions
have failed her
so here she stands
even worse off than she was before
desperately grasping
for wholeness
or healing
or even a glimmer of hope

maybe Jesus…
maybe He will…
be able
to stop the bleeding
of her weary heart
"if only i can get near enough
to reach and touch"

and when she finally
grasps for him
the bleeding stops
the wound is healed
the broken is made whole
relief streaks down
her tearstained cheeks
freedom
finally

he turns and looks
his eyes meet hers
she falls to her knees
in fear and confusion

"daughter"
He tenderly whispers

to the depths of her heart and soul
indescribable intimacy
in the middle of a crowded street

"go in peace"
with a gentle smile upon his lips
knowing
this is what she most deeply longs for

"be freed from your suffering"
and indeed she is
no more bleeding
no more grasping
only love

and in the midst of
her bleeding
and grasping
and healing
i am reminded
of my need
for the same
reminded
of the open wound
of my insecurity
of my grasping
for value and affection
when only One
offers the touch

that will bring wholeness
and freedom

so there is an invitation
for me
to a new life
of indescribable intimacy
and freedom
with the One
who calls me his "son"
with the One
that whispered me into being
and longs for
wholeness
and freedom
for me

if i will let go
of <u>all</u> of the ways
of my grasping heart
and just reach out
for the edge of his robe

pray that i have the courage
 to reach out
like the woman

groaning

o groaning
you wear many faces
today you are loneliness
yesterday you were longing
last week insecurity and inadequacy
and before that struggle, sadness, and hurt

you are a constant companion
always present in some form or another
at times visible and recognizable
and at times hidden and buried deep within
so that i can hardly tell you are there

you walk with a purpose
open up something deep inside me
create fertile soil in my vulnerable heart
you expand my soul
hastening my becoming

you bring me low when i'm too high
make me smaller when i'm too big
you empty me of self when i'm full of it
and meet me tenderly when i'm bruised or broken

you open me up
making me receptive to true presence
you accomplish a purpose
that only a Dreamer could possibly dream up

sometimes i run from you
sometimes i ignore you…or try
and sometimes i embrace you as a long lost friend
which is exactly what you are

o groaning
you wear many faces
work your work in me

heart

Before the beginning there was a Heart
And this Heart was the substance of God
It came from the very core of who God was
And was the very essence of God
from before the beginning
Through His Heart God created all things
Without it nothing received the life-blood of God
This Heart was the source of true *shalom*
Its blood gave us the ability to see
To see the depth of the Heart in spite of all darkness
Because the darkness is unable stop its beating
And God ripped His Heart from His very chest
And He transplanted that Heart into one like us
Wrapping it in flesh and bones and giving Him
a face and a name
And God's Heart lived with us,
He walked with us, talked with us, laughed,
and cried with us
And we saw what God's Heart looked like
It was pumping with the blood of grace and truth

hide and seek

just when i think
i have a handle on you
"i've got you now"

you slip away…
i lose my grip
on the me i thought i was

and am wonderfully left
grasping at thin air
again

hiding

i heard your steps
and was seized with fear
but why?

then your voice—
come out, come out wherever you are

but i didn't even know i was hiding
i had become so used to my surroundings
that i thought they were normal
i thought they were my home—
            where I belonged

so subtle was the cover
that i thought it was a part of me
who i actually was

until you called
            and i saw
                        where i was

you knew all along
and you wanted me to know
but i had been deceived
into thinking i was found
when i was still hiding

home

a beautiful house
        but not yet my home
can it ever be?
and what is the magic that bridges
                        the gap
        helps make
                           the leap

time?
        living?
              being?
                  dwelling?

will dwelling someday turn this house into a home?
or shall i be forever homeless
        an alien and stranger…in a distant land.

You are my home.
as i dwell in You
        i become at home wherever i am.

make your home in me
        and i will make my home in you
forever

music

just a piece of wood
hand-picked with love for its possibilities
unique, like no other
    yet without life

carved and crafted with great intention
sanded and smoothed, hollowed and finished
with great care
    yet still without life

unable to play on its own
unable to make the music
for which it was made
    without the Breath

the Breath of the Maker
Breath that will fill it with life
and allow it to be what and who it really is
    to sing the song it was made to sing

so breathe divine Breath
bring to life that which you have so carefully made
that your tune may resound all through your creation
    adding another instrument to the great symphony

for if you do not give it breath
just a piece of wood is all there will be
and it is the music we long for
    for your music is life

outside

looking in
from beyond the circle
from behind the playground fence
at the connectedness
        the interaction
        the common life
        that is not so common
and me
        alone
        a distant observer
                          outside
wondering
        what it will take
when it might be a possibility
to get in the gate
and how to get there
from here
but for now outside will have to do

peniel

here i am
on a distant shore   again

away from all that i hold dear
          except for the One who holds me
here by choice, but not particularly my own
in the solitude comes a wrestling
a struggle
what is it that has hold of me? or who?
this grip that will not let go
          until it accomplishes its purpose in me
          whatever that is

what is the purpose?
why am i in this lonely place?
if i knew maybe i could go free
but the wrestling is not finished
it has not finished freeing me
from something I didn't even know i was
bound by

great good is being accomplished in this struggle
a brokenness that comes only from strong and
tender hands
and brokenness seems to be the goal
it will leave its mark on my heart and soul
a mark showing me who i really belong to
leaving me with a glorious limp
a reminder of all still yet to be done in me

so here i am
on a distant shore   again

pieces

a piece at a time is how it comes
and where
          does
                    it
                              all
                    fit?
and how?

can i see the picture again? So i'll know.
if not i'll have no clue of where each one fits   or me.
making sense of the pieces
without the picture
                              seems an impossible task
false assumptions
          rabbit trails
                    wrong turns
now i see it
no i don't
waiting…
          for the next piece to be given
waiting…
for all to fall into place   in time
doubting…
          in the midst of the jumble
can i see the picture again? so i'll know.

i need to know to my depths the beauty of it all
i need to know the beauty of the pieces   and trust
because a piece at a time is how it comes

prayer

a gentle hand on my face
a soft whisper in my ear
a warm and intimate embrace
a face filled with affection
eyes dancing with delight
a heart overflowing with love
a beautiful song sung over me
a tender kiss upon my lips
prayer

real

i thought i knew me
but the me i thought i knew
wasn't really me at all
just another clever disguise—an illusion
a person that really doesn't exist
a creation of my own deepest needs and fears
it was the person i thought i needed to be
in order to be valued
in order to be someone worth loving
but how does someone who really does not exist
hold any value at all?
except from this fickle and fleeting world

living a lie
to gain applause and approval
the false for the false
under the guise of true
why is it so hard to tell the difference?
to see and recognize the real—and the not real?
as long as the false is present
the true is hidden
it can't be lived
and what is the process of discovery?
how is the imposter unmasked?
how do i see the real face underneath?
the naked truth?

wear a mask long enough
and you forget you have it on
it becomes who you are—
or you become who it is
until you realize
until you are awakened—
come home to yourself
isn't that what this life is really about?
becoming—
undressing—
letting go of all you thought you knew
in order to discover the true—
the real
the beautiful
waiting underneath.

rhythm

over and over
year after year
the story is retold and relived

it gives rhythm to life
it assures that no season lasts forever
        until the season of forever lasts

it reminds us that
        light always follows darkness
            arrival always follows waiting
                joy always follows suffering
        and resurrection always follows death

it celebrates seeing
        and becoming
            and breathing
                and living

remembering the story offers perspective
giving us perseverance in the season of pain
enabling us to anticipate the season that follows
helping us look forward to how and when
that season will arrive
allowing us to make sense of our current season

remembering the story offers hope
that its author is worthy of our trust
that its truth will be repeated and celebrated again and again
that its rhythm is one that invites us to dance
to dance the dance of faith to the rhythm of the ages
        and dance
            and dance
                and dance

sharp top

goldfinches on pink and red wildflowers
the constant sound of a mountain stream
a slow walk through a tunnel of trees
sitting on a wooden bridge watching water rush past
deer on the lawn at midnight
wild turkeys on an afternoon walk
lightening from the clouds as the moon shines bright
butterflies and bumblebees going from flower to flower
watching fireflies from the porch at dusk
rocking chairs and long conversations
a stream of tears from the eyes of one captured
        by a great affection
seeing people do what they were made to do
and hundreds of friends coming home
who could ask for more?

sitting in the dark

how long?
is the night

must i sit in darkness forever
waiting for your sun to rise
to show itself through the trees
to come up over the hillside once more

this night is dark and cold
it goes on and on
seems to last to eternity

how long?
until you shine on me
how long?
until i feel your warmth again
how long?
until you come and wipe my tears away

and what do i do until then?
what choice do i have?
i can't hasten your coming

all i can do is wait
and watch
and hope
and know
that soon morning will come

and the one who said "let there be light"
will say the words in my heart once more
and the sun will return to my sky

because it always does

slippery

just when i think i've got you
with both hands firmly gripping
you slip away again so quickly
right through my fingers
and i am swept away
into despair
       where did he come from?
       i didn't even see him coming
       he had no invitation—no cause
       he just came—so quickly
       and stole you away
       where did you go?
and how do i get you back
how do i get back to the light
       where perspective returns
       and all seems right again
       and clear
you certainly are a slippery one
       so easily disrupted
       so easily disturbed
yet hard to hold on to
here one minute
and gone the next
is holding on to you even possible?
or is there something else to hold on to
       more substantial
       more stable
       more
or someone
holding on to me

slow

the pace of this amazing journey
        seems to be lessening as each year goes by
        not from need but from desire
        desire to see, desire to notice,
desire to pay attention
but life continues on
        frenetically around
        passing by on the right and the left
        people on their way to…?
        zipping here and darting there
        rushing to this and racing to that
        a frenzy of activity
        afraid to miss anything
        and yet so much is missed.
the landscape of the journey goes unnoticed
the incredible detail of life is overlooked
invitations to transcendence are passed by

i want to travel at a very slow pace
        looking and longing for depth
        seeing the intricacies of life
        accepting the invitation to sit and watch
        yearning for others to join me
yet few seem willing to walk slowly enough to keep up

small

i need to grow smaller
to grow
smaller
it seems a contradiction
a going against the grain
but so right
striking a chord deep within
a yes at the core of my being
a call
to grow smaller,
and smaller,
and smaller,
until i've grown so much
that i disappear
completely

smile

a sweet sweet song
filled with love and affection
sung with a tender caress

my song to you
the love of my heart
whispered softly in your ear
to bring a smile to your lips

but then a change
a turn of the tables
you spin it around
and let me know the song is yours
sung constantly over me

you pull me close
take me to yourself
sing tenderly in my ear
the song of songs
now the smile belongs to me

st. mary's

there is a man in a garden
that hangs from a tree
protecting and caring for those returned to him
His heart is bursting with love,
but his face is filled with loneliness
He is alone, it seems, as he hangs there
      as people pass by on their way to and
      from who knows where
few if any stop and pay him a visit
so when one finally does, as i did on this day
He gushes with words of affection
"stay with me a while longer," he says
for He knows as soon as i leave i'll forget
      it doesn't make him angry
      it makes him sad
      It breaks his heart
for he also knows, better than we, how we
were made
"stay with me a while longer," he says
once more
      so i do
after a while i ask, "are you lonely Jesus?"
"if you had to depend on me for company
      how lonely would you be?"
"You look lonely…hanging up there on that
tree. why don't i sit with you a while
longer."
for as much as you've done for me it seems
like the least i can do
      and maybe the most as well

"my dear one," says he
"don't you worry about me
i have all of the good sisters to keep me
company."
"they adore me and hang on my every word
      they had lots of practice hearing me
while they were on earth."
"they sing to me day and night a song that
reflects the one i sang over them
      it is a lovely song,
i have one for you, too

but you have trouble hearing it
so you go on about your day

and think fondly of me often
for right now you cannot imagine the
depths of my fondness for you
until you, like the good sisters
sit with me in the garden again
for all eternity

strings

tiny little strings
barely visible
attached to my heart
pulling it from its spacious place

one little tug is all it takes
to turn freedom into captivity
freedom so fragile
is not really freedom at all
only an illusion
a temporary lull

funny how these tiny little strings
have such an enormous pull
taking me to the depths
in moments
there to remain
loosely bound
but bound none the less

until the strings are seen
and named
and cut
freeing me
to a spaciousness
that is durable
and is substantial
and is real

so cut these strings
o Lord
and allow me to live
free

that left a mark

it was not invited
and at the time not welcomed
but nonetheless it came calling
bursting through the door
barging into my settled life
turning everything upside down
wounding me to the bone
leaving a deep mark
both upon and within
one that has taken up residence inside
entering my very bloodstream
it will never leave
it is a part of me now
a companion and guide
willing to teach if i am willing to listen
willing to lead if i am willing to follow
life as it was before
has ceased to exist
nothing will ever be the same
it is not bitterness
it is reality
i am forever different
in an incredibly painful
but very good way

thinkin'

"As the heavens are higher than the earth, so are my ways higher than your ways and my thoughts than your thoughts."

Did you know…
That before anything was created you were a thought in my mind?
A thought that brought a smile to my face and joy to my heart
That when I made you—I made you fearfully and wonderfully?
I formed you with great care and intention to be a beautiful expression of my love and care and creativity?
That I molded you and shaped you into the incredibly unique person that you are? And that no one else in all eternity will ever express me the way you do. You are special—of infinite value to me
That when I think of you it brings great delight to my heart?
I love to hear the sound of your laughter and I weep to see the pain of your heart
That I think about you often?
I think about you waking and
I think about you sleeping
I think about you working and
I think about you playing
I think about you dancing and
I think about you mourning
I think about you full and
I think about you empty
I think about you all the time—
I just can't get you off my mind
That when I say my thoughts are higher than yours it includes my thoughts of you? I long for you to see yourself as I see you; to think about yourself as I think of you. If you did your thirst, the deepest longings of your heart, would be truly satisfied and "your soul would delight in the richest of fare."

So "Come, all who are thirsty…"

thinking out loud

maybe...?
what if...?
do you think that...?

beyond the words
   and beneath
   a wrestling
   a wondering
     and wandering

trying and searching
longing and reaching
straining
to find
to be found

to arrive at my destination
to be home

tilt-a-whirl

back and forth
to and fro
here then there
round and round
where will it finally stop?
      and when?
how will i know when to get off?
when my world comes to rest once again?
when i've stopped spinning?
      stopped being so dizzy and restless
      stopped swaying and swinging
      settled in to what this life will be
i'm ready to get off
get my feet back on solid ground
but the ride is not over yet
so for now i just hang on

undone

years and years of hard work
diligently putting it all together
piece by piece
thinking all is well
progress is being made

but then you come
and scramble the whole picture
leaving pieces scattered everywhere

smiling lovingly
as i sit in the middle of the mess
knowing that i don't know
knowing that i'm undone
and thinking to yourself
now that's progress

unknowing

the older i get the more i know
that i don't know
and when i come to know
that i don't know
then i know
something worth
knowing

unnamed

watering the seed
      and watching
      and believing
      and hoping
      and waiting
      for it to grow and emerge from the soil
      so it can be seen
what sort of thing is this that grows within?
      in the deep rich darkness that is not dark to you
      knowing that there is growth within
      but not knowing quite what it is
      knowing and not knowing
trusting the seed to do its job
      it knows what it is to become
      and when
and so i water
      and watch
      and believe
      and hope
      and wait
      and know
      and not know

why the tears?

overwhelming longing
for deep connectedness
ache of the heart
      a joyful pain
      a tearful smile
knowing and being known
delighting and being delighted in
cherishing and being cherished
just a taste of
love unspeakable

window

older and simpler they sat
enjoying each other's company
       amongst the orange and red
they had been together for some time
you could tell by the ease with which
       they talked and sat together
as they placed the meal on the table
they did what they must've done
       a thousand times before
       but still with a freshness
they stopped and bowed and prayed
the words were as simple as they were profound
"our father we thank thee"
and that was all
and they meant it

the stone lies
on its side
rolled away
easter has
uttered an
invitation *Rise Up! Come out! Enjoy the light of
new life!* but instead we sit befriending the dark
tomb content with despairing—inertia or gravity
has taken
hold so we
sit and mope
in the dark
even though
the stone lies
on its side
rolled away
(by Jim Branch)

Prayers

O God, our Heavenly Father, who created us beautifully and wonderfully, may we always look to You for our value and worth, remembering that we are a unique expression of your infinite love, care, and creativity. Help us, O Lord, to see ourselves as you see us—objects of your extravagant love and tender affection. Through Christ. Amen.

By your cross O Lord, you show the extravagance of your love for us. Love than knows no limits…no boundaries. Love that pours down upon us from every wound of your beloved Son. More love than we could ever ask for or imagine. When we are tempted to doubt the depths of your heart for us, let our eyes immediately look to Jesus crucified—and may all doubt be taken away. In His name. Amen.

O Lord, help me to really believe. Help me to really believe that your heart for me is good. Help me to really believe that nothing can separate me from your love. Help me to really believe that you will do what you say you will do. Help me to take you at your word. In the name of Jesus. Amen.

Dear Jesus,
   Speak to me during this day about the story you are telling, the story I was made for. Open my eyes, Lord, to the ways that story is being lived out in the events and circumstances of this day. Show me how all that happens to me this day echoes Your larger Story if only I will keep my heart focused on you. In your name I pray. Amen.

Father, write yourself upon my heart and life—that I may be an open book about you, so that others might read of your unending love on every page. In the name of Jesus, the author and perfecter of our faith. Amen.

O Loving God, who breathed me into being, breathe your Divine Breath in me again this day—that I might be filled with your life and guided by the winds of your Spirit. For the sake of your Son. Amen.

Thank you Lord, that you see me as holy because of the gift of your Son. Help me to celebrate the holiness you have given me by being wholly yours this day. Amen.

O Lord my God, how I long to recapture the purity and joy of the Garden—when I was able to stand before you (and others) naked and unashamed. That, indeed, is what I was made for. But this side of heaven that is not my reality. My reality is filled with fear and shame; hiding and covering—terrified that I will be exposed, found out, not enough. How I genuinely long for true communion with you; total vulnerability; deep trust—to be fully known and fully loved. Have mercy on me! Amen

Lord Jesus, give me the grace and the strength and the courage to take off that which I use to cover myself; and to clothe myself only and always in you alone. Amen.

Lord Jesus, forgive me when my bleeding and wounded heart causes me to grasp for life and relief from any and every source available. Instead, help me to reach only for you—that I might touch the fringe of your robe and find healing and wholeness for the brokenness of my heart and soul. In Your Name I pray. Amen.

Lord God, give me open hands and not clenched fists as I walk with you and for you in the midst of this day— that I might be able to live with a true sense of freedom from the need to grasp desperately for love and value from those I come into contact with. For Jesus' sake. Amen.

Lord God, be the delight of our hearts, even as we are the delight of yours. And help us to leave behind all thoughts, actions, and attitudes that do not reflect the beauty of that delight. May everything else pale in comparison with the passion we have to be truly yours. In the name of Jesus. Amen.

O Lord, our God, so much of this life is lived *in between*; between the now and the not yet, between arriving and departing, between birth and death and rebirth, between growing up and growing old, between questions and answers. Help us not to live only for some distant day when the *in between* will be no more, but help us to step into the mystery of that sacred space here and now—knowing that it will be a place of genuine change and true transformation.

Lord Jesus, Help me to trust you fully in the midst of this life that seems so chaotic and unsure at times. Give me, this day, a firm place to set my feet as I walk toward you through this ever-changing world. Amen.

Father, forgive us when we think that life is more about what we are doing than about who we are becoming. Help us to remember that more than anything else you want our hearts. Allow us to give them to you fully, that we might receive yours in return; changing us more into the likeness your Son Jesus. In His name we pray. Amen.

O God, who existed before all things, draw near to my heart today as I draw near to yours. Grant that as we are together during this time—as well as this day—I will know of your presence to the very core of my being. Let me experience the intimacy with you that I was created for. In the name of Jesus, the Word made flesh. Amen.

O Lord, as we spend time with you and your Word this day, let us hear the words of your Ancient Song; and let us listen closely for the Song of God that rises in our hearts. In Christ. Amen.

Everything in all of creation, O Lord, is a unique song of yours. And when we sing our song—that song that is buried deeply within each of us—we are indeed being who we were made to be. We are in harmony (*shalom*) with the voice of our Maker. Help us to sing our song (Your song) clearly and fully this day. In the name of Jesus. Amen.

My God and Father, Lord of the dance, allow me to see this day and this moment for what it really is—an invitation to dance the dance of life and faith with the One who made me. May I dance this day with joy and passion, knowing that there will never be another one just like it. In the name of Jesus I Pray. Amen.

Lord God, draw me out on the dance floor of life this day and fill my ears and heart with the beautiful music of Your great affection. Give me such an awareness of your presence that my feet just can't be still. Dance with me as I dance with you. Amen.

Father,
    Allow the soil of my soul to be a place that is fertile and receptive to all that you desire to plant in my heart. Tend it carefully and nurture all that has sprung up in me that is of you; that I may be a garden of your delight. Through Jesus. Amen.

Grow your good grace in me O God. Make me receptive to the ways that you water and tend this garden of my heart. Prune me where I need pruning, nurture me where I need nurturing, weed me where I need weeding, and care for me tenderly where I need your tender care. I love you, O Gardner of my soul. In the tenderness of Jesus. Amen.

Our Father, help us to see you today in all that we come into contact with, knowing that you use ordinary things to give us an extraordinary sense of your presence in our lives. In the name of Jesus. Amen.

Lord,
    Help me walk slowly and deeply with you through the hours and minutes of this day—that I might find all of you that is to be found within it. Allow me not to miss you because of hurry or busyness, but let me sense the fullness of your presence in each moment. Slow down both my feet and my heart that I might be more present to you as I go about my normal activities. In the Name of Jesus I pray. Amen.

Father, I know my wounded and broken places oh so well. At times they can consume me and keep me from being able to hear your voice. Help me to see my pain as an invitation to know you more intimately rather than a reason to doubt the goodness of your heart. Help me to know that through my pain you desire to accomplish something very good in me. In the name of Jesus, the author of our salvation, who was "made perfect through suffering." Amen.

Father, heal my wounds and make them a source of life for others; as you did with your Son Jesus. In whose name we pray. Amen.

O Lord our God, help us to be faithful to gather what you have provided for our hearts and souls this day—that we may feed on you and live. In the name of Jesus, the bread of life. Amen.

Lord Jesus, thank you that you are present in the midst of the broken pieces of this day. May we find you there as we gather them up and may it help us to trust both your provision for us, as well as the goodness of your heart. Amen.

O God, our Father, Creator of all that is, give us the courage to wrestle with the questions you ask us rather than jumping to some immediate answer—thereby cutting off any possibility of real growth or struggle. Help us stay in the question long enough to hear what it is you have for us there. In the name of Jesus. Amen.

O Lord our God, help us to live our lives with the faith and courage necessary to live by love and not by fear. Forgive me when my seeing and my thinking get so distorted that I allow fear to control me and make me its slave—even when I don't fully realize it. Seize my heart and soul with your perfect love in such a way that it drives out all fear and gives me the freedom to truly love, rather than manipulate, those in my life and world. In the name of Jesus. Amen.

Lord Jesus,
    Help me to hear your words, "Take courage! It is I. Don't be afraid." and to believe them in the deepest places of my heart. Help me to live my life by those words this day. For your sake and by your Spirit and in your name. Amen.

O Lord my God, thank you that you keep track of all my sorrows. That you have collected my tears in your bottle. That you have recorded each one in your book. And that all the tears I've shed cannot begin to compare with the ones you shed for me. Amen.

Thank you, Lord Jesus that you wept. Thank you that you are a God who weeps—that our sorrow and sadness bring tears to your eyes as well. Thank you that you hold us, as well as all our tears, in the palm of your pierced hand. Amen.

Lord Jesus, give us the grace and the strength and the courage to follow your invitation downward—to the place where there is only you and nothing else. In your name and for your sake we pray. Amen.

O Lord our God, may something new be born in us this day, as well as this season—this season where we celebrate your birth into this cold and cruel world. This season where we rejoice over your amazing arrival to live among us; to give us light and life and hope and peace. We pray this in the Name of Jesus. Amen

Made in the USA
Lexington, KY
27 June 2012